A Tenth of Hydrogen

A Tenth of Hydrogen

Daphne Rock

ISBN: 978-0-9539815-4-0

First published November 2011
by Corundum Press
83 Montrose Avenue,
Leamington Spa,
Warwickshire.
CV32 7DR

Printed in Britain by:
imprintdigital.net
Seychelles Farm,
Upton Pyne,
Exeter
EX5 5HY
www.imprintdigital.net

A Tenth of Hydrogen

Daphne Rock

ACKNOWLEDGEMENTS

The pamphlet collection *Is It Now* was published by Hearing Eye in 2006. 'Crawl Space' is from the sequence *Easy to Miss*, Corundum Press, 2001. 'Peter Bellinger Brodie' is in the anthology *This Life on Earth*, and 'The Beach at Trouville' in *Lancaster Litfest Poems 21*. Other poems first appeared in the magazines *Artemis*, *Dream Catcher*, *Envoi*, *The Interpreter's House* and *Staple*.

Edited by Rosemary Norman, Felicity Rock
and Jenny Vuglar with a foreword by Mario Petrucci

Corundum Press

CONTENTS

Earlier Uncollected Poems

EDITORS' NOTE

There are small adjustments made by the editors to four poems. They are the footnotes to 'Field Trip' and 'Suddenly', the asterisks between the second and third sections of 'Crawl Space', and the subtitles Bones and Skin in 'Land'.

We'd like to thank Mario Petrucci for our online discussion while he worked on the foreword, and Kate Foley and Lyn Moir, without whom two poems would have been missing from this collection.

**Rosemary Norman, Felicity Rock, Jenny Vuglar
August 2011**

According to Ian Fleming, you only live twice: once when you are born, and again when you look death in the face. Fleming attempts to encapsulate a critically human moment for the human condition in general, but unwittingly provides a most suitable epitaph for a very particular South London poet. To confront death so unflinchingly, indeed to face death down until that mutual gaze – infinitely held by a mostly indifferent Reaper – is forced to yield up a gasp of delicate or sublime imagery, is to have mastered something essential in the making of self. For this to have been communicated, so effectively, into poetry redoubles Daphne Rock's achievement.

When I first met Daphne at *The Open Poetry Conventicle* in the late eighties, she struck me as a person entirely co-extensive with her poetry. She lived the attitudes her poems encapsulate. Run by the charismatic Carol Fisher, the *Conventicle* met on the last Sunday of every month at the Dance Attic in Putney Bridge Road. This joint workshop-reading enterprise was a nub in the emergent poetry workshop scene, one I have never seen reported in more 'official' accounts of the genesis of London poetry workshops (whose preoccupations north of the river are not entirely justified). The *Conventicle* provided a formative milieu for such poets as myself, Rosemary Norman, Katherine Gallagher, Johan de Wit, Adele David and the inimitable Timothy Gallagher, while early guests included the likes of Gavin Ewart, Ian McMillan, Liz Lochhead and Grace Nichols. Whatever corpus of poetics had its origins in Putney, Daphne was undoubtedly one of its vital organs.

The distinctive manner in which Daphne would draw smoke from a cigarette reified the qualities of her poetry: elegant yet direct, intelligent, open to approach. A surface calm sheens the work, but belies her profound and often edgy appetite for intensity, her unstinting exploration of meaning and the apt representation of meaning. Daphne's attention to detail, along with a fascination with geology and 'deep time' (that is, time on a cosmic scale), inform her output through and through, fusing with an acerbic streak, a dark seam of wit, a deceptively plain yet quarried precision. Moreover, she seemed immune to what Milan Kundera, contemplating Flaubert, describes as "Modern stupidity... the *nonthought of received ideas*". Daphne did little to identify herself with flock or herd. No ox-eye or poppy, then, but a singular orchid.

Among the many things I learned from Daphne, Carol and other *Conventicle* members, is that dishonesty poisons the discussion of poetry: be as constructive as you can, naturally; but never disingenuous. In that spirit, I do wonder about Daphne's (very occasional) embracing of the stock phrase, and whether her tone, for all its astringent efficiency, sometimes verges on an unmodulated transparency of address, a slightly mannered relentlessness? No poet is without flaw, of course, but in *A Tenth Of Hydrogen* Daphne's are mostly relegated to the faintest of whiffs, having become rarefied (it would seem) through the finality of her subject matter operating more completely upon her vigorous sensibility. Still, one would not say these poems are so much fireballs as fine cinders that smoulder unquenchably with a darker heat. Or, put differently, using the opposing element, this poetry shows us that quiet, less ostentatious waves forge landscapes as much as the noisily crashing surges and tides. Daphne's is a closely-formed, insistent voice that cuts into the mind many (not entirely settling) harbours.

Daphne died "still deep with words" ('Poets Die'), surviving her first bout of bowel cancer to set this crucial stratum within the slim profile of her oeuvre. Her debut, *Waiting for Trumpets* (Peterloo, 1998), does not define her, quite; *A Tenth Of Hydrogen* goes a long way to fleshing out a fuller poetic definition of what she was. This combines her Hearing Eye publication, *Is It Now* (2006), with the terse poetry composed deep in debilitating illness that restricted her to snatches of writing lasting just ten or fifteen minutes at a time. 'Police Tape' was Daphne's very last poem. The third and final section of the book gathers earlier uncollected poems in such a way as to seem to cause the collection to turn its back on itself, breaking off its staring match with illness and death in order to flick more discursively over the rugged limestone hills of family, living, history and personality. By turns wry and shocking, these latter poems drive us again among ravines and chasms characterised by danger. If what Daphne reaps here is occasionally grim, the book's movement into this terrain is nevertheless apt, returning us to quotidian epiphanies already altered and shrouded by the searing opening poems, only to discover, once more, death, murder and decay. Even when turned, Daphne cannot be made to flinch. Caught in that space "between dark and dark" ('Sleepless') – a void which rather brings Lucretius to mind – her gaze settles again, and at last, upon cosmic time. The editors have put together a wise and suggestively ordered collection.

It feels both joyous and vaguely distressing to read Daphne's words knowing she is no longer bodily here to speak them. The posthumous situation evokes a strangeness: that eternal question of what it is that art can represent of its artist, or literature of its author. Poets must always depart their poems, whether they be alive or dead in actuality; but Daphne has met this question with more than words and minerals. To imitate the closing words of 'Years Later': poetry is not a grave, not yet; we can always come back. Something of Daphne moves shrewdly behind this collection, a determination that is restlessly earthy even as it reaches towards transcendence. What is important here is not that Daphne Rock is, at her best, both memorable and incisive, but that she can be so in her own particular way. *A Tenth Of Hydrogen* is, for me, the collection in which Daphne's lifelong commitment to observation and knowledge, that yearning named in 'Is It Now' as "green soul", is most apparent. It deserves readers.

Mario Petrucci
July 2011

from *Is It Now*

If I Miss Anything

If I miss anything it will be skies,
that one has been washed
in dilute charcoal, a half brush of pink trim,
sinking into the edge of wherever you happen to be
only you don't expect to
miss anything

from the time you were dressed in
a flannelette gown, flat on your back when everything
      was sky,
at least between the rain hood and the tucked up
satin edge blanket framing the day;

and growing up with nothing taller than terraces,
all arranged on floury cumulus
while late night coaches took you on
impenetrable journeys to empyrean heights,

also trees which broke up firmaments
into pieces cut too small for heron wings
and school which never told
why such red-yellows flowed
out from the dying sun, leaving suddenly,
nor why the night went blue
some winters. Rainbows too
lost you in prism, spectrum and refraction,
such mysteries puffed up the deep vault
for your delight.

Burial takes all, steals the sky twice over:
sometimes you should lie
flat on your back above the burying earth.

Last To Die

Surely an end to events,
at least those of the known world
where men sailed, rocked on the tabletop of earth,
turning the wheel sharply to beat the sun
at its own game. The known world
where Eden lurked in hiding and God
sat in the cool of the garden.

Still no saying that the world is round –
people have been wrong before,
star-gazing, mapping the oceans, it is
possible the world's elliptical
tipping about all over the place.

When you trip, fall off,
you are the last to go,
eyes stone-dead for future deaths
while explorers beat across seas and
you are silent. Too late to inform
anyone of the latest astronomical findings,
head first you fall, like the sinner in an old Doom,
wordless you crash into the stars.

Is It Now

In St George's Hospital

Expecting the rushing meteor, the asteroid
large and dark, plunging from a cloud,
a suddenness and some brilliance,
hard to settle for
the catheter bag gasping on the floor, murky with urine
and the tubes marking flesh,
a world all body. If only
someone had painted the walls
into the unreal loom of gases, an eye
for the next world, dark or blazing.

In the night
a magic lantern of shapes
drifts around, light returning
and fading.
Is it now? How wraiths merge into moonlight
and dawn takes days to break.

Let my green soul sit on my lips
reaching for light while the body sings
of dark stone, of flint walls.

In The Old Books

In the old books they used pennies
shutting out the sun. Now the hand
quietly angles the heel
to tuck eyelid into socket
behind the screen.

Let eyes discover new ways of seeing. We suppose
there are no more stars
rolled in to explain mysteries, rather
the veiled eye turns mineral, takes on crystal forms
which burn with pristine habits

already voyaging beyond time:
new skies, new continents.

Through The Crack In The Door: Cavell Ward

Imagine you see
spring faces, time-stranded,
floating in and out of
sudden shafts of gloom, one more step
is enough,
turns you to memory, nudged about
by shadows and the back-face
of a door, you will never
forget the retreat and that line of
faces sunk just below the surface
calling you into
years without end, you turn
one more time, growing pink and lined,
winter-faced, feeling the earth.

Years Later: Mewslade Bay, Gower

Wild garlic, you can scarcely
pick feet through this star-white frothing
and it is as before. The track is as before,
the sea crushed into breakers mounting high, only she
is not as before. Always a hard descent,
funnelling through limestone blocks,
rocking stones, sudden drops – now
pebbles stretch almost to the sea's mouth,
old legs are driven on
like the blown foam, speckled on sleeves, on rock pools,
cloaking perilous deeps;
she is wound with wraiths and shadows
drifting and teasing, as if they could
drag her back, shadow ropes to bind her
with thin half words, reminder of
the glorious leaping from stone to stone,
catapult across canyons,
chiding and teasing while
she ages, the voices fall.

Old knees crack,
a lunge for handholds, fingers slide
over the sharp rock, and poles spin, giddying the day;
fingers flailing for grip, a voice in the stomach
stifled at the mouth, stiffens the spine, *go back*,
beyond the sea-litter, the spent foam,
springs trickling, the wet conglomerate,
the ill-placed boulders, god knows

these were not the legs she began with
on those bright mornings. Out there
breakers advance and if she falls now,
if she falls they will certainly
treat her like bladder wrack, like a torn limpet,
to be washed up in pieces like the crab,
which she deserves, old fool, still tottering
on stone glass-smooth, harried round in the swell.

She grasps that common sense she once
clothed herself in, up and down the beach
watchful for each beloved, counting, counting,
vigilance forced on like a cold skin.

She's there. Sands to centre her. Seas
making in over the flat shore,
tides without mind, her goal
eaten up by water. Around her
ghost voices, drift of children's laughter,
her pockets full of apples...

                              But then the retreat,
grudgingly, waves filled with witches from the deep, calling
return, return. Hands strung with sugar kelp
tangle her feet.

Time to save herself
she hauls her body upward. Knuckles bleed
red into sandstone. This place is not a grave,
not yet. She can always come back.

Ear Stopped

Each day you throw off waking dread. Set to.
Keep house, put out clean towels, watch
trees grow, fall, seed and rise again.
You stroke the arm that never yet
has failed commands. Sirens do not acquaint you
with *their abhord abode.*

Odysseus going home, chose
to stop every eare
with sweet soft waxe so close that none may heare
a note of all their charmings.

But they sing close, O yes, they sing
in the night, catch you off guard
with telephones that yield no message.
They take on new tones, out there on the road
where metal jars on metal. As well, then
your men to bind you foote and hand
sure to the Mast.

No time, not yet, you cry, for listening.

Quotations from Chapman's *Odyssey* Book Twelve.

Easy To Forget

Easy to forget
the dead tucked into every earth corner,
easy to forget they line our world,
can't remember
crying over great grandfathers, over
the bones which once made a dance of life,
can't believe
fear shrieked silently in their anxious heads, laughter
layered like leaves in winter cried to keep
unbelief at bay, the living
pretending to be immortal,
until the shadow stalks, and the dead
take on a patina of remembrance.

So many then have kept their secret,
refused to imagine death which has
travelled in disguise, better myths
of Styx, of Lethe, Hell even
than millions gone to history, all cancelled,
time and its ending.

Forever lives like a dead star
left to light a brief memorial, no need
to suffer with the dead, their fate is
to slip into ending with the crowd
until the world is stifled, body-full.

Endoscopy

Lest I should be mislaid they tied
a label round my wrist:
name sex and number
ready to be returned if
crazed with terror I took flight:

but I played good, left it too late
to leap from bondage, cameras wandered
down my oesophagus and further
someone reflects upon
such a long stomach, then –
open, close please, some tiny secateurs
snipped pieces from my secret inner life
while I bled finger nails into my hand
and hoped to die.

This film I will not watch except in
thicketed corridors of night
where horrors wander, where I swallow dragons,
struggling as they wind
into and up and round and round and round

Christmas Day 2005

A time for the present
and not the present of santas and stars
crushed in old wrapping
but a moment too small to measure
as we close down tomorrow
shut the door on yesterday
only the light rising behind trees
its brightness blurring the edges
deepens the panoply of stars turning
the tiny pulse of now
into the brilliant burn of being here
where ending and beginning have no space.

The Third Who Walks With Us

The glaze of late September is falling on firs
and pooling grass still rain damp; out of sight
the chalk road rides high to Guildford.

There are little gold spots on leaves
and you leap stiles, stride out,
the sun lights you.

The village wanders in crooked fieldways,
gardens trimmed for show
straggle out and fade, grass overtakes them:
soon we join the North Downs Way.

The donor, whoever he was, leaps stiles with you
and walks the North Downs Way
having given all that the dead can give:
the one with no shadow
always walking with you.

Field Trip

When you took us to see the Norber erratics
I was amazed by their numbers:
all these swept across the Dales
by glaciers and dumped on limestone pavements,
for some reason now lost in geological time.
You said (we had made our sketch map
of one black boulder and we had measured angles
which told of the likely direction
from which the rocks had travelled)
they were still restocking the fields
further down the valley
after the pestilence.

The erratics stock-still on the high ground,
hardly altered over centuries
and centuries again before they change to
a beach of wind blown sand.
Quite different from the fields, emptied overnight,
the imprint of beasts smudged on the green grass.

Spring 2001. To control an outbreak of Foot and Mouth disease
farm animals in affected areas were culled.

Black Dog Walking

Terezin 1996

Hana has painted a black dog walking.
She died in Auschwitz, nineteen forty-four.
She was fourteen. That much is certain.

I find myself thinking for her,
invading her secrets,
inventing her words

for the worst is silence,
no clues to nightmare
nor to awakening.

The child artist
captures no ambiguity –
that must be composed

of nothing more
than a black dog,
ears pricked, waiting for walking.

Death Assemblage

Ploughing the Somme Fields
year after year, the corn full-headed,
ears fat and prosperous,
blades throwing a bleached bone, a splinter
distorted with rust which has bled
and crusted into a metal scab.

Now they have exposed a mass grave
of assorted bone. Buttons bulbous with accretions.
It makes the Six O'clock News:
the authorities are concerned to discover
whether like lies with like
and who can be named
with his regimental buttons,
his vestigial shoulder tabs.

Millions of years past
the mountains shifted, swept
dead shell to rock grave,
ammonite and brachiopod, crinoid,
they died apart
and then brushed shoulders, landed fixed
immutably with strangers.
Geologists label this a death assemblage.

The authorities are busy
counting buttons, scraping off deposits, sorting and
    dividing.
How many buttons make a man?
Say six. That means

plots must be cleared for twenty-eight found men.
Perhaps the hearts
of some descendants can be cheered,
grandad found at last. But dead.
Of course research could show
a shell-disturbed collection, may include
the enemy, our boys beside the Hun.
A death assemblage.

In Life

This field now under plough, earth burial for you;
it was all raspberries that summer,
all plush purple. Twice we walked to the farmhouse
carrying punnets, light then weighted,
layered thick with berries.

Gate gone to hedge now guarding winter wheat
and you, your dust gone to the ocean, sea burial;
each time – passing the field, where the road rises
and the old raspberry pitch tips down the hill
(further than we expected that hot summer,
the long cane rows and no-one on site) –
each time green shoots blur into raspberry fields
where finger-stained with fruits you are
printed plain beneath new crops.

Last Poems

Poets Die

Poets die still deep with words,
ribbons of lines, verses
like unstitched tapestries and whole pages
not yet set. They lie unfathomed,
crowded into jars and button tins,
beads waiting for stringing. Listen –
you hear them, small clinks of glass and pearl,
rolling around, not into emptiness, they wait
to make a way to the sun, quickened
even in earth.

Suddenly

Karachi 18th October 2007

Imagine life snapped out,
no warning. No air on the face,
no sound. No
imagining. No loss of
last faint pressure from
receding fingers,
all preparations lost.

You went too fast they say.
I never said... O but you did,
your whole life said.
Forget the dust, the blood, hold to
the love, the love.

At least 139 people were killed on this day in a bomb attack on a
motorcade carrying Benazir Bhutto. She was assassinated two
months later.

Next

You know how the earth sank, weighed down with
the burden of ice, impossible to
shrug off that oppressor, and
you know how it still rises, slowly, slowly,
after the melt. You know.

And how you still feel,
shoulders wrenched, above the horizon
the lost stars, you will stand
again, before taking off, before feet
shake free of the long familiar ground.

Sleepless

These charcoal hours with their thin fingers
drawing night through glass
and the long wait for sullen days
they drag at the arms and separate
the smallness. Too little strength to unite day and dark.
The body slips into those winding coils
clouded and grey and there's the fight
to turn back, into the
little morning star and the hollow
gap between dark and dark.

Police Tape

From the road a gleam on the hill,
closer the grass is flat, there
by the pony paddock. They nudge at
the faint warmth where her blood slowed.
Curious they try the gate, wound with
police tape. The stretcher path has
bruised heather and harebell. No one
lays memorials, or has grieved with posies,
she chose well enough, ponies to sing her
through the country park, silent over footpaths.

Earlier Uncollected Poems

Ellen At Munday's Hill

Her high visibility vest billows yellow wings
as she planes and tilts high on the silver sand.
She is joy taking off
with her red hard hat askew, her ponytail flying;

Wellington boots clammed with the Gault clay
she slips, riding the sand slope
arms wide with delight, covering
sixty-five million years in seconds, head over heels
laughing and gathering nodules
which spark against the white light.

Her pockets are heavy with fossil woods
annual rings diamante with bracelets of fool's gold.

Joyous, she is printed on every plane of the vast pit
like the sun which once
coaxed life from the world,
nurtured small puffs of oxygen to grow
lungs and fingers and wings.

Today she is the sun.

Father

1. Birth

Eleven thirty. She is almost born,
Elbowing her way through.

Father outside the door. After midnight
his birthday too.

The babe
jumped too soon, impatient,
butted the source of air and
roared into day's end.

Father in the shadows.
No birthday cards that year. Later
father and daughter, regarding
that half hour
would consider that it did not count too much,
but oh, what a world that was, that gap
between November nights, even now
she waits for midnight, bearing him past his dead years,
so close, just missing though.

2. Death

They kept her in the dark. Shielded her from
his sad garden, nothing green
breaking the winter ground.

A man of small histories –
board school boy where
for excellent attendance
his prize was *Tom Brown*.
Britannia ruled, he stood up for the King
and talked of "gunboats":
probably he was teasing, so tender he was
with hedgehogs and young birds, even
the tortoise which devoured his lettuces
gently admonished and sent off replete.

At least she has that –
netting the strawberries and
rubbing out the eggs of Cabbage White,
but no-one told her he was dying
would not live to hold the child she carried.

Charitable to think
they expected more time. Tell her after the birth:
time for him then to hold
the child to his thin breast.

Even now
she expects him to turn up with
first peas of the season, a bag of King Edwards and
fresh radishes.

Barometer and Peanuts

I am my grandfather.
Now that I own a barometer.
Each day I pause in the hall. Tap tap
with an imperial finger.
Great grandfather fought
in the Crimea. He sits his imperial horse
above the turn of the stair.
As my grandfather I note
that the time on the grandfather clock
coincides with my half hunter tucked
in a waistcoat pocket. All is set fair.

I am my grandfather. Half way down the stairs
he looks out from his frame,
tucked in by his watch chain.
I tell him, we have lost the Crimea
and the clock was sold.
Somebody somewhere says
that man on a horse, who is he?
Tap tap. For those who will become me
I fill the bird feeders
with peanuts. All is set
for change.

For my cat Mimi, died November 2006

No more exploring the dank leaves
blown up on borders, settling in the wind,
or seeking water from green cups
set deep in ivy, no starting
at the fox's pad past the back gate,
sudden retreat to the warm undergrowth of
      carpet and curtain
and your mild eyes insistent for care, the retreat now
a perpetual place of safety,
old blanket by a door, uncertain
until death becomes your need.

You leave a shadow, a cold space,
leaves blowing all across your familiar path.

A Further Call To Arms

Remembrance Sunday 1997

These old men should be in the dry,
they'll catch their death, they try –
marching with a swing – and how could they refuse
to obey this Order, though they'd scarcely choose

to tramp Whitehall at the eleventh hour, being
eighty plus and seeing
visions of God knows what disinterred
from layers of living on, moments that occurred

before they'd known much
stuff hidden in memory, raw to the touch.
They ought to be out of the rain,
if they must be conscripted, again and again,

give them mufflers, greatcoats, roadside fires
lest they die to the sound of bugles, rather than
    angel choirs.

Grandmother, Mother And The Letter

"Gurney Ward, nineteen twenty-five,
my own dear
little girl"

(my mother, twenty-five years old,
puts this letter by)

"Thank you. There is nothing
a mother appreciates so much
as the confidence of her children"

(Mother has written
that she loves the boy next door)

"Don't let him give you money.
Trust in God, I am sure
it is cheaper at home without Nurse and me"

(he has gone to work in the Argentine:
Mother cannot bear it)

"My bit of sunshine, you stay,
don't go far away, on your own,
I'll be home in a wheelchair soon"

(Mother returns the ring
to a central American port)

"Keep a good heart dearie:
keep straight and all will be well.
I will send you ten shillings soon"

(Mother marries another,
my father, two years on)

"If I cannot walk
Dad must get me a chair;
I shall take it into the garden"

(a quiet wedding, after she dies,
and just the one letter, in pencil)

The Beach At Trouville

after Monet

Odette thinks I am reading the newspaper,
I have marked my gloves with print
and hold my head at an angle fit for headlines.

Oh, but I heard her breathe faster,
saw the lace shiver on her breast.
Behind my deckchair he walked, eyes locking hers.
Odette is perfectly confident,
under the hot black gown I am dead;
my blood dead; I am silly with trivia. Fool.

So prim, maman sits in her black,
see, already she has smudged
print on her gloves. That tells
how things lie beneath her bombazine...
I don't expect much, pearls
would have a hard time getting past those lips.

I can smell the steam of lust, penetrating
bodice seams, corsage,
the fruit on her hat is beaded with it.

The old, they always forbid us
their own excesses. She won't comprehend
my love, like a clean tide,
sweeping sand-smooth as the flesh beneath my blouse,
cooling the scorch of his eye.

Any comment from me, she will tap teeth on her
    reddened lip,
measure the breathing, eyes
(oh, bluer than mine, ever)
blank as a coin.

That finger running around her neck,
pinching for spare flesh.
Ha, let her scheme. She won't find
eyes burning through her parasol.
Her tides ebb. You see,
I read her like a book.

Now that her father is dead
I must make arrangements,
Georges perhaps. Vineyards, almost my age and
robust, I am told, in bed.

Odette, read girl, read
while you can.
We shall return soon to the farm.

Sea Change

She'd worn elastic belts,
old girdles, smocks and pleated skirts
and taken whiskey in prodigious doses:

she'd lifted groceries and sacks of coal
and made a show of gluttony, downed chips
and buttered buns and sweets and sticky cakes

she'd cursed and fallen down the stairs one night

she'd felt the bastard kick and surge inside her,
she'd bound her belly, punched it, sat
in hot baths, cold baths, caught a chill or two,

her nightmares told her tales of monster children,
she planned a smothering, a strangulation,
when she was sure the time had come she ran

down to the river, coughed the child out: fright

prevented her, not love, from burial,
she took some driftwood, laid the marble babe
as offering before the ship of death

which bore it on the water, river god
snatching so quick and fast she had no time
to close the eyes, she was relieved, amazed

to feel so little guilt, such cold delight.

Martyrs

The sons meet in heaven,
they are thin, clap hands to the chest
where explosives kept them warm,
examine each other, enquire
did you know how small you were
under the death belt and ask
who cries for you but they know no-one cries
or perhaps the infidel told to love enemies
but they hope parents observe their crowns of glory,
proclaim they gave birth to martyrs and saints.
The sons are proud to be dead. Secretly
they long to live again, see the sun rise,
go uncrowned about their business.

Sun Rises On Death Row

Late dawn lights the Ohio sky, Don takes his morning rec.
sees sudden sunrise. A universe lit for him:
whatever his sins.
His sky-square turned to sun and now he may
also catch sunset. As the season turns or earth turns
sun notes arrival and departure:
all the slow progress of the courts, of death
should leave at least a chance
to be caught up again by the sun, over the earth's rim,
    like a free man.

Rec. hours are set, no swerving, no appeal,
do they know light shortens in September
a privilege not listed, the heart's delight,
keep quiet then, keep eagerness locked up,
watch for the swift drop
at the end of the day.

The Turkey's Song

I almost remember dark sweat-boxes,
lying beside dead friends, hardly believing
we had ceased to be our own masters,
nowhere to put our feet, the air foul –

we had heard almost since birth
how to respect the lesser beings
with whom we share the planet:
I only speak for turkeys of course –
but for us every creature carries
a duty to harmony.
I cannot understand
how they live with the sight of us,
imprisoned, hostage to viruses,
even think of feeding on us. I hesitate
to call them cannibals, though
we have always believed
each is made in God's image, I admit some
prefer Him like a bird, but that is
the way of birds, even the ant and
the tick beneath my feathers
are permissibly gods.

Now I almost remember
seeing them shackled into boats
but who stole them, gave them
their terrible ways I do not know.
But it was not us.

British Rail Have Finished Clearing Up The Debris...

scrubbing blood off stone.
If you've ever scrubbed blood
you'll know how thin it lies
on surfaces, pink water:
apologetic, almost, for being visible.

Rivers of life live in secret:
we pretend they are solid, pretend
weapons make holes we can plug
with body-filler.

Everyone should scrub blood
once in their lives.
Circle the lakes without bounds:
trap platelets in a floor cloth
soon dry. Brown crust and flake.
Only when first spilled will you remember
its slop around your wrists,
its quantity.

Bringing Home The Sweet Potatoes

Mud stuck to them. Thick skinned.
Cleaned under the hot tap. Dirt in the crevices
scarring orange flesh. Beneath is gold and good.

Mud smudges under nails, runs diluted down
pinkish fingers. A little water clears
but the mud of Israel leaves grit on the tongue.

The Last Man On Flat Earth

Each evening he walks in the meadow
where sheep follow their appointed cycle,
birth, feed and fatten,
woolgather, die, sacrifice
their atoms to soil,
one way or the other.

The dogs are his companions,
they surge, low on the ground, after scents
of badger and fox.
Into the forestry
where oaks fend off
conifers and the wild cherry.
Where cones have been nibbled to death
by wood creatures. Blackberry flowers and fades
under a leaf sky. Tough grass
and branches dry for the fire;
reeds sit deserted
on the drained hill.

Fox reigns, ducks die, species turn tail
while he pushes back centuries
walking the hill. He is
the last man on flat earth.

His dogs light on carrion,
rook stripped, are urged past
badger setts, hidden under
scrub whose roots
toughen an old motte.
He sees the heron spot
a feast in the river.

There are no echoes of soldiers
stripping the castle bones
only calls, and wind whipping
surplus material over the edge.

He finds order,
the last man on flat earth.

Storm Over Essex

Mid June. Thunder crashes about.
We shelter in the nave. Note windows,
ill made jigsaws of old glass;
we are directed to study
apses turned foursquare as masons learned
to square the circle, fitting curves to cubes.

Lightning creeps through Saxon double splays.
Flits over Roman tile, outside
rain darkens travertine and the pebbledash
of glacial outwash. Flint knapped and squared,
puddingstone for luck. All kinds.

Washed out land, never an ashlar for neatness.
Great rubble walls stamped black with gravel clusters.
Churches built of allsorts, the spoils of Rome
serve for the gaps. All kinds of god
in these walled histories.

Tegulae died with Rome. Eight hundred years
before the Saxons mastered skills of tile;
there are *quern* pieces, finger printed by
women grinding corn. Precious Purbeck
smashed from gravestones. Iron slag.

Stone museums, full of voices,
women with shattered *querns* and men
quarrying for heroes.
The same electric sky above the Blackwater,
piercing the nave with light.

Taynton Quarry

Cows note resentfully our ease with the gate.
In the field beyond
sheep form ranks, then scatter
at the tramp of field boots.

The October sun
has scoured the sky of shadow;
overhead hawthorns hang
seed heads for plucking.

The larger blocks sit solid, grass bearded.
The little quarry's yellow-warm, abandoned.
There's pluck and feather cavities, this grainy rock
needed hand splitting. Then cart and water journeys
to Taynton graveyard, to Oxford
for Christ Church cloisters, Chapter House and spire.

No hands to split and cart now. Geologists
hammer out their samples. Barns fall
into stone heaps. The slabs of time grow thin:
hundreds of years
between the hammers and the quarrymen.
Millions of centuries
between them and the warm Jurassic seas.

Crawl Space

Time is not always the best place to look for history
        Roger Osborne

I should not have assumed
that the guide had considered my limitations
or that the rules had been kept
regarding safety. Certainly I was in error
expecting the path to be cleared in advance
of hazards I could not even imagine.

Going down a mine I bragged: I had complained
of theme park history, corners rubbed off:
I knew of the millions of years
during which lead sat in the rock
unseen because there were no eyes, and I knew
the *old man* mined in darkness, rough tooled,
with dynamite to blast a way ahead,
and water always a pest, to say the least.

I was even expecting a thrill, an insight,
I with my clean nails and soft flesh
thought time would oblige, smooth the way,
allow me the present while I explored the past.

I did not imagine
the passage would drop knee high,
crowding the shoulders,
rock clutching and squeezing
like a man greedy for possession
forcing breasts down on the limestone teeth,

knees cracked, slipping in blood,
the dark ahead a black pit,
no knowing where it might end,
this sharp embrace.
All the handbooks, explanations
and carefully measured diagrams had failed.

***

Now time slips away, its parting gift the terror of return,
in the hill I hear the regular drip-fill of water;
turning is hard,
the rock assaults me, a known fear:
I clutch now and the rock yields.
I hoist myself back by my fingertips,
flat, face so close to the rock
I can lick the lime into my dry mouth.

***

Light at the end of the tunnel. I catch myself
in platitudes. After all,
they must have been used to it.

Groaning Tor Level: Via Gellia: Derbyshire

Land

The first part of an unfinished poem 'The Reliquary: a tour of
bones and skin'

1. Bones

The inmates eye us up despite their empty sockets,
    draw us in, two by two.
Claiming us. Already
cold creeps into our fingers, we find ourselves posed
head high like the giraffes
whole giraffes, heads on the ceiling bent to observe.

*and of every living thing of all flesh, two of every sort shalt
thou bring into the ark...every creeping thing that creepeth
upon the earth...two and two of all flesh wherein is the
breath of life*

No breath of life here. We alone cause the dust
to be stirred, bone dust shifting and falling as we expel
gentle breaths of wonder.

They have come in their scores
from the halls of knights and adventurers.
We feel ourselves unravel, skin shrunk away, our
    bone exposed,
not so bright as we imagined,
not white like the reindeer there who starred in
    Santa's film,
cast off and shot, bones bundled into this Ark
boiled they say to make a decent end.

The earth also was corrupt before God...
and behold, I will destroy them...

We never expected, never found, gopher wood,
no stalls for pairs no perches for the birds,
no salt sea wind. This Ark preserves
those already dead.

Sculpted in bone the heads of elephants sit ear to ear,
nod bonily at us. They are mended and dusted and
      the air
as pure as when they wandered blindly
out on Mount Ararat or under prairie grass.

Already our soft parts tremble.
The stuff beneath the skin makes ghosts of us,
we stamp a little on the concrete floor, move to be alive.

Now we are mobbed by antlers, row upon row,
mobbed by ranks of rib cages barrelling across plains
      of decking.
We are mobbed by memories, lessons taught in schools,
 battlefields; bodies split,
come apart so simply. Reassembled here where all
      breath is gone.

Skeleton giraffes now, vertebrae a necklace of carved beads
strung between metal stands. Straw pokes from a neck
carelessly parted from its little head.

Our fingers check a pulse for
vessels of blood which navigate our journey, which
might prove our departure. Or did we become dreams
when the door of the warehouse shut, wasting in the
      cool air.

2. Skin

Fancies of Lenin, waxy in the tomb (the long queue,
    how we waited
hour after hour in the snow under a dead sky and
    the guards
needling us with their eyes) but here
bone on bone, we watch, do not worship.

Here a white tiger, did Noah discover two, before
all the fountains of the great deep were broken up and the
    windows of heaven were
opened, not knowing
a future King would kill, stain the beautiful coat, skin him,
find him unsuitable for palaces and
land him here. He stands without frills on a bare board.
White satin gently creased with pale folds of dust.

The Victorians too shot tigers, this one, extinct,
is lovingly preserved, he lies surrounded
by earthly pleasures, grasses, blue sky.
No dust in his glass case, no moth.
He is almost breathing, sniffing the far air,
his heart almost moving rhythmically the still skin.

Everyone eager now to shift stuffed trophies. Stately walls
with pale patches soon to be transformed with modern art.
Here is a great space hired for storage, a new model
    ark to confront
the wickedness of man ... great in the earth.
Creatures sit in stillness, breath stopped as if indeed
the end of all flesh is come before me, here
only DNA is found immortal.

The Zoo donated Guy the Gorilla. He's tucked away,
lips frozen in a smile.

It is strong here, the desire to be stilled, preserved from
the earth filled with violence. We shiver as blood slows,
air thins, connective tissue locks, we force walking, one
    foot before another,
slow. Lungs shrink.

This was to be fun, lighthearted, but the heart
beats raggedly, we are drawn to dying.

With acknowledgements to The Natural History Museum and their
stored collection in Wandsworth, London.

Quotations in Italics from *The Jerusalem Bible*.

Peter Bellinger Brodie

1815-1897: Rector and geologist

I imagine him in an old felt hat, booted and caped,
wet with dawn mist as he tapped out
an insect from long solitude in the Blue Lias:
the first man to set eyes on so beautiful a thing,
evidence of evolution tucked in his cassock.

Bible at hand and
in the spare moments between sermons
he studied evidence of Warwick under ice,
under deep seas and spattered with volcanoes.

Keen clerics everywhere
roamed rocks and chasms, stood tip toe on cliffs
down which might tumble Genesis:
the heavens and earth and all the host of them.

Peter Bellinger Brodie, clerk in holy orders,
a man of God with science in his trust.
His *History of Fossil Insects* stayed
this side of heresy – safely, when he died
they said *he loved God's world.*

A Tenth Of Hydrogen

They say: a tenth of all bodies
contains that pristine hydrogen,
a gas passed down five thousand million years...
...light and inflammable,
and nothing to show until
it burns to water...

...you look normal enough,
not even a gleam or spark
winking and dancing as when
it burst from the Big Bang
to spin and recompose,
then pass through unguessed ancestors:
who would you choose
to share your beginnings, world's eternity?
and who will host those secrets
once meant to die with you?

Out of your hands in any case
and there – it flies off,
possibly touched with faint tincture of newness,
a mote to settle on
the eyelashes of the child following,
inheriting matter which was never young.